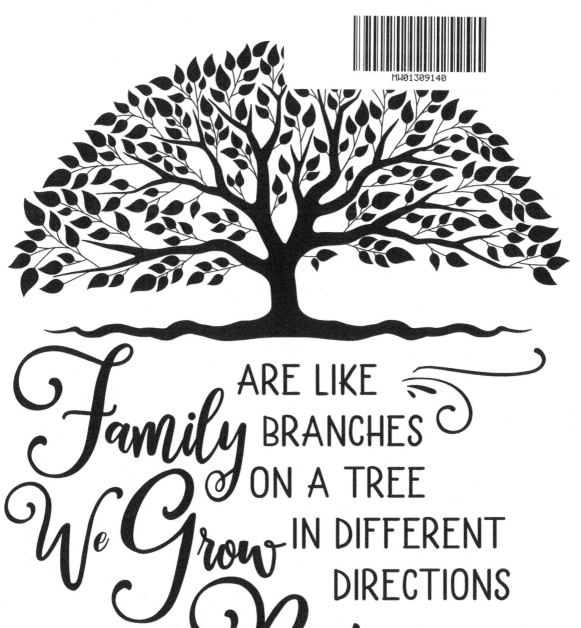

Family ARE LIKE BRANCHES ON A TREE
We Grow IN DIFFERENT DIRECTIONS
YET OUR Roots REMAIN AS ONE

GUEST BOOK

FAMILY REUNION GUEST BOOK
FAMILY ROOTS

©2019 GUESTBOOKS FOR EVERY OCCASION | ALL RIGHTS RESERVED

No part of this publication may be reproduced, distributed, or transmitted in any form or by any means, electronic or mechanical, including photocopying, recording, or by any information storage or retrieval system.

....
FAMILY REUNION

....
LOCATION

....
DATE   TIME

NAME ....

BIRTHDAYS .... ANNIVERSARY ....

ADDRESS ....

....

HOME .... MOBILE ....

EMAIL ....

CHILDREN & BIRTHDAYS ....

....

FAVORITE MEMORY ....

....

....

....

....

NAME ....

BIRTHDAYS .... ANNIVERSARY ....

ADDRESS ....

....

HOME .... MOBILE ....

EMAIL ....

CHILDREN & BIRTHDAYS ....

....

FAVORITE MEMORY ....

....

....

....

....

NAME ....
BIRTHDAYS .... ANNIVERSARY ....
ADDRESS ....
....
HOME .... MOBILE ....
EMAIL ....
CHILDREN & BIRTHDAYS ....
....
FAVORITE MEMORY ....
....
....
....
....

NAME ....
BIRTHDAYS .... ANNIVERSARY ....
ADDRESS ....
....
HOME .... MOBILE ....
EMAIL ....
CHILDREN & BIRTHDAYS ....
....
FAVORITE MEMORY ....
....
....
....
....

NAME ....
BIRTHDAYS .... ANNIVERSARY ....
ADDRESS ....
....
HOME .... MOBILE ....
EMAIL ....
CHILDREN & BIRTHDAYS ....
....
FAVORITE MEMORY ....
....
....
....
....

NAME ....
BIRTHDAYS .... ANNIVERSARY ....
ADDRESS ....
....
HOME .... MOBILE ....
EMAIL ....
CHILDREN & BIRTHDAYS ....
....
FAVORITE MEMORY ....
....
....
....
....

NAME ....

BIRTHDAYS .... ANNIVERSARY ....

ADDRESS ....

....

HOME .... MOBILE ....

EMAIL ....

CHILDREN & BIRTHDAYS ....

....

FAVORITE MEMORY ....

....

....

....

....

NAME ....

BIRTHDAYS .... ANNIVERSARY ....

ADDRESS ....

....

HOME .... MOBILE ....

EMAIL ....

CHILDREN & BIRTHDAYS ....

....

FAVORITE MEMORY ....

....

....

....

....

NAME ....

BIRTHDAYS .... ANNIVERSARY ....

ADDRESS ....

....

HOME .... MOBILE ....

EMAIL ....

CHILDREN & BIRTHDAYS ....

....

FAVORITE MEMORY ....

....

....

....

....

NAME ....

BIRTHDAYS .... ANNIVERSARY ....

ADDRESS ....

....

HOME .... MOBILE ....

EMAIL ....

CHILDREN & BIRTHDAYS ....

....

FAVORITE MEMORY ....

....

....

....

....

NAME ....
BIRTHDAYS .... ANNIVERSARY ....
ADDRESS ....
....
HOME .... MOBILE ....
EMAIL ....
CHILDREN & BIRTHDAYS ....
....
FAVORITE MEMORY ....
....
....
....
....

NAME ....
BIRTHDAYS .... ANNIVERSARY ....
ADDRESS ....
....
HOME .... MOBILE ....
EMAIL ....
CHILDREN & BIRTHDAYS ....
....
FAVORITE MEMORY ....
....
....
....
....

NAME ....
BIRTHDAYS .... ANNIVERSARY ....
ADDRESS ....
....
HOME .... MOBILE ....
EMAIL ....
CHILDREN & BIRTHDAYS ....
....
FAVORITE MEMORY ....
....
....
....
....

NAME ....
BIRTHDAYS .... ANNIVERSARY ....
ADDRESS ....
....
HOME .... MOBILE ....
EMAIL ....
CHILDREN & BIRTHDAYS ....
....
FAVORITE MEMORY ....
....
....
....
....

NAME ....
BIRTHDAYS .... ANNIVERSARY ....
ADDRESS ....
....
HOME .... MOBILE ....
EMAIL ....
CHILDREN & BIRTHDAYS ....
....
FAVORITE MEMORY ....
....
....
....
....

NAME ....
BIRTHDAYS .... ANNIVERSARY ....
ADDRESS ....
....
HOME .... MOBILE ....
EMAIL ....
CHILDREN & BIRTHDAYS ....
....
FAVORITE MEMORY ....
....
....
....
....

NAME ....
BIRTHDAYS .... ANNIVERSARY ....
ADDRESS ....
....
HOME .... MOBILE ....
EMAIL ....
CHILDREN & BIRTHDAYS ....
....
FAVORITE MEMORY ....
....
....
....
....

NAME ....
BIRTHDAYS .... ANNIVERSARY ....
ADDRESS ....
....
HOME .... MOBILE ....
EMAIL ....
CHILDREN & BIRTHDAYS ....
....
FAVORITE MEMORY ....
....
....
....
....

NAME ....
BIRTHDAYS .... ANNIVERSARY ....
ADDRESS ....
....
HOME .... MOBILE ....
EMAIL ....
CHILDREN & BIRTHDAYS ....
....
FAVORITE MEMORY ....
....
....
....
....

NAME ....
BIRTHDAYS .... ANNIVERSARY ....
ADDRESS ....
....
HOME .... MOBILE ....
EMAIL ....
CHILDREN & BIRTHDAYS ....
....
FAVORITE MEMORY ....
....
....
....
....

NAME ....

BIRTHDAYS .... ANNIVERSARY ....

ADDRESS ....

....

HOME .... MOBILE ....

EMAIL ....

CHILDREN & BIRTHDAYS ....

....

FAVORITE MEMORY ....

....

....

....

....

NAME ....

BIRTHDAYS .... ANNIVERSARY ....

ADDRESS ....

....

HOME .... MOBILE ....

EMAIL ....

CHILDREN & BIRTHDAYS ....

....

FAVORITE MEMORY ....

....

....

....

....

NAME . . . .
BIRTHDAYS . . . . ANNIVERSARY . . . .
ADDRESS . . . .
. . . .
HOME . . . . MOBILE . . . .
EMAIL . . . .
CHILDREN & BIRTHDAYS . . . .
. . . .
FAVORITE MEMORY . . . .
. . . .
. . . .
. . . .
. . . .

NAME . . . .
BIRTHDAYS . . . . ANNIVERSARY . . . .
ADDRESS . . . .
. . . .
HOME . . . . MOBILE . . . .
EMAIL . . . .
CHILDREN & BIRTHDAYS . . . .
. . . .
FAVORITE MEMORY . . . .
. . . .
. . . .
. . . .
. . . .

NAME ....
BIRTHDAYS .... ANNIVERSARY ....
ADDRESS ....
....
HOME .... MOBILE ....
EMAIL ....
CHILDREN & BIRTHDAYS ....
....
FAVORITE MEMORY ....
....
....
....
....

NAME ....
BIRTHDAYS .... ANNIVERSARY ....
ADDRESS ....
....
HOME .... MOBILE ....
EMAIL ....
CHILDREN & BIRTHDAYS ....
....
FAVORITE MEMORY ....
....
....
....
....

NAME ....
BIRTHDAYS .... ANNIVERSARY ....
ADDRESS ....
....
HOME .... MOBILE ....
EMAIL ....
CHILDREN & BIRTHDAYS ....
....
FAVORITE MEMORY ....
....
....
....
....

NAME ....
BIRTHDAYS .... ANNIVERSARY ....
ADDRESS ....
....
HOME .... MOBILE ....
EMAIL ....
CHILDREN & BIRTHDAYS ....
....
FAVORITE MEMORY ....
....
....
....
....

NAME ....
BIRTHDAYS .... ANNIVERSARY ....
ADDRESS ....
....

HOME .... MOBILE ....
EMAIL ....
CHILDREN & BIRTHDAYS ....
....
FAVORITE MEMORY ....
....
....
....
....

NAME ....
BIRTHDAYS .... ANNIVERSARY ....
ADDRESS ....
....

HOME .... MOBILE ....
EMAIL ....
CHILDREN & BIRTHDAYS ....
....
FAVORITE MEMORY ....
....
....
....
....

NAME ....
BIRTHDAYS .... ANNIVERSARY ....
ADDRESS ....
....
HOME .... MOBILE ....
EMAIL ....
CHILDREN & BIRTHDAYS ....
....
FAVORITE MEMORY ....
....
....
....
....

NAME ....
BIRTHDAYS .... ANNIVERSARY ....
ADDRESS ....
....
HOME .... MOBILE ....
EMAIL ....
CHILDREN & BIRTHDAYS ....
....
FAVORITE MEMORY ....
....
....
....
....

NAME ....
BIRTHDAYS .... ANNIVERSARY ....
ADDRESS ....
....
HOME .... MOBILE ....
EMAIL ....
CHILDREN & BIRTHDAYS ....
....
FAVORITE MEMORY ....
....
....
....
....

NAME ....
BIRTHDAYS .... ANNIVERSARY ....
ADDRESS ....
....
HOME .... MOBILE ....
EMAIL ....
CHILDREN & BIRTHDAYS ....
....
FAVORITE MEMORY ....
....
....
....
....

NAME ....
BIRTHDAYS .... ANNIVERSARY ....
ADDRESS ....

....

HOME .... MOBILE ....
EMAIL ....
CHILDREN & BIRTHDAYS ....

....

FAVORITE MEMORY ....

....

....

....

NAME ....
BIRTHDAYS .... ANNIVERSARY ....
ADDRESS ....

....

HOME .... MOBILE ....
EMAIL ....
CHILDREN & BIRTHDAYS ....

....

FAVORITE MEMORY ....

....

....

....

NAME ....
BIRTHDAYS .... ANNIVERSARY ....
ADDRESS ....
....

HOME .... MOBILE ....
EMAIL ....
CHILDREN & BIRTHDAYS ....
....
FAVORITE MEMORY ....
....
....
....
....

NAME ....
BIRTHDAYS .... ANNIVERSARY ....
ADDRESS ....
....

HOME .... MOBILE ....
EMAIL ....
CHILDREN & BIRTHDAYS ....
....
FAVORITE MEMORY ....
....
....
....
....

NAME ....
BIRTHDAYS .... ANNIVERSARY ....
ADDRESS ....
....
HOME .... MOBILE ....
EMAIL ....
CHILDREN & BIRTHDAYS ....
....
FAVORITE MEMORY ....
....
....
....
....

NAME ....
BIRTHDAYS .... ANNIVERSARY ....
ADDRESS ....
....
HOME .... MOBILE ....
EMAIL ....
CHILDREN & BIRTHDAYS ....
....
FAVORITE MEMORY ....
....
....
....
....

NAME ....
BIRTHDAYS .... ANNIVERSARY ....
ADDRESS ....
....
HOME .... MOBILE ....
EMAIL ....
CHILDREN & BIRTHDAYS ....
....
FAVORITE MEMORY ....
....
....
....
....

NAME ....
BIRTHDAYS .... ANNIVERSARY ....
ADDRESS ....
....
HOME .... MOBILE ....
EMAIL ....
CHILDREN & BIRTHDAYS ....
....
FAVORITE MEMORY ....
....
....
....
....

NAME ....

BIRTHDAYS .... ANNIVERSARY ....

ADDRESS ....

....

HOME .... MOBILE ....

EMAIL ....

CHILDREN & BIRTHDAYS ....

....

FAVORITE MEMORY ....

....

....

....

....

NAME ....

BIRTHDAYS .... ANNIVERSARY ....

ADDRESS ....

....

HOME .... MOBILE ....

EMAIL ....

CHILDREN & BIRTHDAYS ....

....

FAVORITE MEMORY ....

....

....

....

....

NAME ....

BIRTHDAYS .... ANNIVERSARY ....

ADDRESS ....

....

HOME .... MOBILE ....

EMAIL ....

CHILDREN & BIRTHDAYS ....

....

FAVORITE MEMORY ....

....

....

....

....

NAME ....

BIRTHDAYS .... ANNIVERSARY ....

ADDRESS ....

....

HOME .... MOBILE ....

EMAIL ....

CHILDREN & BIRTHDAYS ....

....

FAVORITE MEMORY ....

....

....

....

....

NAME ....
BIRTHDAYS .... ANNIVERSARY ....
ADDRESS ....
....
HOME .... MOBILE ....
EMAIL ....
CHILDREN & BIRTHDAYS ....
....
FAVORITE MEMORY ....
....
....
....
....

NAME ....
BIRTHDAYS .... ANNIVERSARY ....
ADDRESS ....
....
HOME .... MOBILE ....
EMAIL ....
CHILDREN & BIRTHDAYS ....
....
FAVORITE MEMORY ....
....
....
....
....

NAME ....
BIRTHDAYS .... ANNIVERSARY ....
ADDRESS ....
....
HOME .... MOBILE ....
EMAIL ....
CHILDREN & BIRTHDAYS ....
....
FAVORITE MEMORY ....
....
....
....
....

NAME ....
BIRTHDAYS .... ANNIVERSARY ....
ADDRESS ....
....
HOME .... MOBILE ....
EMAIL ....
CHILDREN & BIRTHDAYS ....
....
FAVORITE MEMORY ....
....
....
....
....

NAME ....
BIRTHDAYS .... ANNIVERSARY ....
ADDRESS ....
....
HOME .... MOBILE ....
EMAIL ....
CHILDREN & BIRTHDAYS ....
....
FAVORITE MEMORY ....
....
....
....
....

NAME ....
BIRTHDAYS .... ANNIVERSARY ....
ADDRESS ....
....
HOME .... MOBILE ....
EMAIL ....
CHILDREN & BIRTHDAYS ....
....
FAVORITE MEMORY ....
....
....
....
....

NAME ....
BIRTHDAYS .... ANNIVERSARY ....
ADDRESS ....
....

HOME .... MOBILE ....
EMAIL ....
CHILDREN & BIRTHDAYS ....
....
FAVORITE MEMORY ....
....
....
....
....

NAME ....
BIRTHDAYS .... ANNIVERSARY ....
ADDRESS ....
....

HOME .... MOBILE ....
EMAIL ....
CHILDREN & BIRTHDAYS ....
....
FAVORITE MEMORY ....
....
....
....
....

NAME ....
BIRTHDAYS .... ANNIVERSARY ....
ADDRESS ....
....
HOME .... MOBILE ....
EMAIL ....
CHILDREN & BIRTHDAYS ....
....
FAVORITE MEMORY ....
....
....
....
....

NAME ....
BIRTHDAYS .... ANNIVERSARY ....
ADDRESS ....
....
HOME .... MOBILE ....
EMAIL ....
CHILDREN & BIRTHDAYS ....
....
FAVORITE MEMORY ....
....
....
....
....

NAME ....

BIRTHDAYS .... ANNIVERSARY ....

ADDRESS ....

....

HOME .... MOBILE ....

EMAIL ....

CHILDREN & BIRTHDAYS ....

....

FAVORITE MEMORY ....

....

....

....

....

NAME ....

BIRTHDAYS .... ANNIVERSARY ....

ADDRESS ....

....

HOME .... MOBILE ....

EMAIL ....

CHILDREN & BIRTHDAYS ....

....

FAVORITE MEMORY ....

....

....

....

....

NAME ....

BIRTHDAYS .... ANNIVERSARY ....

ADDRESS ....

....

HOME .... MOBILE ....

EMAIL ....

CHILDREN & BIRTHDAYS ....

....

FAVORITE MEMORY ....

....

....

....

....

NAME ....

BIRTHDAYS .... ANNIVERSARY ....

ADDRESS ....

....

HOME .... MOBILE ....

EMAIL ....

CHILDREN & BIRTHDAYS ....

....

FAVORITE MEMORY ....

....

....

....

....

NAME ....
BIRTHDAYS .... ANNIVERSARY ....
ADDRESS ....
....
HOME .... MOBILE ....
EMAIL ....
CHILDREN & BIRTHDAYS ....
....
FAVORITE MEMORY ....
....
....
....
....

NAME ....
BIRTHDAYS .... ANNIVERSARY ....
ADDRESS ....
....
HOME .... MOBILE ....
EMAIL ....
CHILDREN & BIRTHDAYS ....
....
FAVORITE MEMORY ....
....
....
....
....

NAME ....
BIRTHDAYS .... ANNIVERSARY ....
ADDRESS ....
....

HOME .... MOBILE ....
EMAIL ....
CHILDREN & BIRTHDAYS ....
....
FAVORITE MEMORY ....
....
....
....
....

NAME ....
BIRTHDAYS .... ANNIVERSARY ....
ADDRESS ....
....

HOME .... MOBILE ....
EMAIL ....
CHILDREN & BIRTHDAYS ....
....
FAVORITE MEMORY ....
....
....
....
....

NAME ....
BIRTHDAYS .... ANNIVERSARY ....
ADDRESS ....
....
HOME .... MOBILE ....
EMAIL ....
CHILDREN & BIRTHDAYS ....
....
FAVORITE MEMORY ....
....
....
....
....

NAME ....
BIRTHDAYS .... ANNIVERSARY ....
ADDRESS ....
....
HOME .... MOBILE ....
EMAIL ....
CHILDREN & BIRTHDAYS ....
....
FAVORITE MEMORY ....
....
....
....
....

NAME ....
BIRTHDAYS .... ANNIVERSARY ....
ADDRESS ....
....
HOME .... MOBILE ....
EMAIL ....
CHILDREN & BIRTHDAYS ....
....
FAVORITE MEMORY ....
....
....
....
....

NAME ....
BIRTHDAYS .... ANNIVERSARY ....
ADDRESS ....
....
HOME .... MOBILE ....
EMAIL ....
CHILDREN & BIRTHDAYS ....
....
FAVORITE MEMORY ....
....
....
....
....

NAME ....
BIRTHDAYS .... ANNIVERSARY ....
ADDRESS ....
....
HOME .... MOBILE ....
EMAIL ....
CHILDREN & BIRTHDAYS ....
....
FAVORITE MEMORY ....
....
....
....
....

NAME ....
BIRTHDAYS .... ANNIVERSARY ....
ADDRESS ....
....
HOME .... MOBILE ....
EMAIL ....
CHILDREN & BIRTHDAYS ....
....
FAVORITE MEMORY ....
....
....
....
....

NAME ....
BIRTHDAYS .... ANNIVERSARY ....
ADDRESS ....
....
HOME .... MOBILE ....
EMAIL ....
CHILDREN & BIRTHDAYS ....
....
FAVORITE MEMORY ....
....
....
....
....

NAME ....
BIRTHDAYS .... ANNIVERSARY ....
ADDRESS ....
....
HOME .... MOBILE ....
EMAIL ....
CHILDREN & BIRTHDAYS ....
....
FAVORITE MEMORY ....
....
....
....
....

NAME ....
BIRTHDAYS .... ANNIVERSARY ....
ADDRESS ....

....

HOME .... MOBILE ....
EMAIL ....
CHILDREN & BIRTHDAYS ....

....

FAVORITE MEMORY ....

....

....

....

....

NAME ....
BIRTHDAYS .... ANNIVERSARY ....
ADDRESS ....

....

HOME .... MOBILE ....
EMAIL ....
CHILDREN & BIRTHDAYS ....

....

FAVORITE MEMORY ....

....

....

....

....

NAME ....

BIRTHDAYS .... ANNIVERSARY ....

ADDRESS ....

....

HOME .... MOBILE ....

EMAIL ....

CHILDREN & BIRTHDAYS ....

....

FAVORITE MEMORY ....

....

....

....

....

NAME ....

BIRTHDAYS .... ANNIVERSARY ....

ADDRESS ....

....

HOME .... MOBILE ....

EMAIL ....

CHILDREN & BIRTHDAYS ....

....

FAVORITE MEMORY ....

....

....

....

....

NAME ....
BIRTHDAYS .... ANNIVERSARY ....
ADDRESS ....
....
HOME .... MOBILE ....
EMAIL ....
CHILDREN & BIRTHDAYS ....
....
FAVORITE MEMORY ....
....
....
....
....

NAME ....
BIRTHDAYS .... ANNIVERSARY ....
ADDRESS ....
....
HOME .... MOBILE ....
EMAIL ....
CHILDREN & BIRTHDAYS ....
....
FAVORITE MEMORY ....
....
....
....
....

NAME ....

BIRTHDAYS .... ANNIVERSARY ....

ADDRESS ....

....

HOME .... MOBILE ....

EMAIL ....

CHILDREN & BIRTHDAYS ....

....

FAVORITE MEMORY ....

....

....

....

....

NAME ....

BIRTHDAYS .... ANNIVERSARY ....

ADDRESS ....

....

HOME .... MOBILE ....

EMAIL ....

CHILDREN & BIRTHDAYS ....

....

FAVORITE MEMORY ....

....

....

....

....

NAME ....
BIRTHDAYS .... ANNIVERSARY ....
ADDRESS ....
....
HOME .... MOBILE ....
EMAIL ....
CHILDREN & BIRTHDAYS ....
....
FAVORITE MEMORY ....
....
....
....
....

NAME ....
BIRTHDAYS .... ANNIVERSARY ....
ADDRESS ....
....
HOME .... MOBILE ....
EMAIL ....
CHILDREN & BIRTHDAYS ....
....
FAVORITE MEMORY ....
....
....
....
....

NAME ....
BIRTHDAYS .... ANNIVERSARY ....
ADDRESS ....
....
HOME .... MOBILE ....
EMAIL ....
CHILDREN & BIRTHDAYS ....
....
FAVORITE MEMORY ....
....
....
....
....

NAME ....
BIRTHDAYS .... ANNIVERSARY ....
ADDRESS ....
....
HOME .... MOBILE ....
EMAIL ....
CHILDREN & BIRTHDAYS ....
....
FAVORITE MEMORY ....
....
....
....
....

NAME ....

BIRTHDAYS .... ANNIVERSARY ....

ADDRESS ....

....

HOME .... MOBILE ....

EMAIL ....

CHILDREN & BIRTHDAYS ....

....

FAVORITE MEMORY ....

....

....

....

....

NAME ....

BIRTHDAYS .... ANNIVERSARY ....

ADDRESS ....

....

HOME .... MOBILE ....

EMAIL ....

CHILDREN & BIRTHDAYS ....

....

FAVORITE MEMORY ....

....

....

....

....

NAME ....

BIRTHDAYS .... ANNIVERSARY ....

ADDRESS ....

....

HOME .... MOBILE ....

EMAIL ....

CHILDREN & BIRTHDAYS ....

....

FAVORITE MEMORY ....

....

....

....

....

NAME ....

BIRTHDAYS .... ANNIVERSARY ....

ADDRESS ....

....

HOME .... MOBILE ....

EMAIL ....

CHILDREN & BIRTHDAYS ....

....

FAVORITE MEMORY ....

....

....

....

....

NAME ....
BIRTHDAYS .... ANNIVERSARY ....
ADDRESS ....
....
HOME .... MOBILE ....
EMAIL ....
CHILDREN & BIRTHDAYS ....
....
FAVORITE MEMORY ....
....
....
....
....

NAME ....
BIRTHDAYS .... ANNIVERSARY ....
ADDRESS ....
....
HOME .... MOBILE ....
EMAIL ....
CHILDREN & BIRTHDAYS ....
....
FAVORITE MEMORY ....
....
....
....
....

NAME ....
BIRTHDAYS .... ANNIVERSARY ....
ADDRESS ....
....
HOME .... MOBILE ....
EMAIL ....
CHILDREN & BIRTHDAYS ....
....
FAVORITE MEMORY ....
....
....
....
....

NAME ....
BIRTHDAYS .... ANNIVERSARY ....
ADDRESS ....
....
HOME .... MOBILE ....
EMAIL ....
CHILDREN & BIRTHDAYS ....
....
FAVORITE MEMORY ....
....
....
....
....

NAME ....
BIRTHDAYS .... ANNIVERSARY ....
ADDRESS ....
....
HOME .... MOBILE ....
EMAIL ....
CHILDREN & BIRTHDAYS ....
....
FAVORITE MEMORY ....
....
....
....
....

NAME ....
BIRTHDAYS .... ANNIVERSARY ....
ADDRESS ....
....
HOME .... MOBILE ....
EMAIL ....
CHILDREN & BIRTHDAYS ....
....
FAVORITE MEMORY ....
....
....
....
....

NAME ....

BIRTHDAYS .... ANNIVERSARY ....

ADDRESS ....

....

HOME .... MOBILE ....

EMAIL ....

CHILDREN & BIRTHDAYS ....

....

FAVORITE MEMORY ....

....

....

....

....

NAME ....

BIRTHDAYS .... ANNIVERSARY ....

ADDRESS ....

....

HOME .... MOBILE ....

EMAIL ....

CHILDREN & BIRTHDAYS ....

....

FAVORITE MEMORY ....

....

....

....

....

NAME ....
BIRTHDAYS .... ANNIVERSARY ....
ADDRESS ....
....
HOME .... MOBILE ....
EMAIL ....
CHILDREN & BIRTHDAYS ....
....
FAVORITE MEMORY ....
....
....
....
....

NAME ....
BIRTHDAYS .... ANNIVERSARY ....
ADDRESS ....
....
HOME .... MOBILE ....
EMAIL ....
CHILDREN & BIRTHDAYS ....
....
FAVORITE MEMORY ....
....
....
....
....

NAME ....

BIRTHDAYS .... ANNIVERSARY ....

ADDRESS ....

....

HOME .... MOBILE ....

EMAIL ....

CHILDREN & BIRTHDAYS ....

....

FAVORITE MEMORY ....

....

....

....

....

NAME ....

BIRTHDAYS .... ANNIVERSARY ....

ADDRESS ....

....

HOME .... MOBILE ....

EMAIL ....

CHILDREN & BIRTHDAYS ....

....

FAVORITE MEMORY ....

....

....

....

....

NAME ....
BIRTHDAYS .... ANNIVERSARY ....
ADDRESS ....
....

HOME .... MOBILE ....
EMAIL ....
CHILDREN & BIRTHDAYS ....
....
FAVORITE MEMORY ....
....
....
....
....

NAME ....
BIRTHDAYS .... ANNIVERSARY ....
ADDRESS ....
....

HOME .... MOBILE ....
EMAIL ....
CHILDREN & BIRTHDAYS ....
....
FAVORITE MEMORY ....
....
....
....
....

NAME ....

BIRTHDAYS .... ANNIVERSARY ....

ADDRESS ....

....

HOME .... MOBILE ....

EMAIL ....

CHILDREN & BIRTHDAYS ....

....

FAVORITE MEMORY ....

....

....

....

....

NAME ....

BIRTHDAYS .... ANNIVERSARY ....

ADDRESS ....

....

HOME .... MOBILE ....

EMAIL ....

CHILDREN & BIRTHDAYS ....

....

FAVORITE MEMORY ....

....

....

....

....

NAME ....
BIRTHDAYS .... ANNIVERSARY ....
ADDRESS ....
....
HOME .... MOBILE ....
EMAIL ....
CHILDREN & BIRTHDAYS ....
....
FAVORITE MEMORY ....
....
....
....
....

NAME ....
BIRTHDAYS .... ANNIVERSARY ....
ADDRESS ....
....
HOME .... MOBILE ....
EMAIL ....
CHILDREN & BIRTHDAYS ....
....
FAVORITE MEMORY ....
....
....
....
....

NAME ....
BIRTHDAYS .... ANNIVERSARY ....
ADDRESS ....
....
HOME .... MOBILE ....
EMAIL ....
CHILDREN & BIRTHDAYS ....
....
FAVORITE MEMORY ....
....
....
....
....

NAME ....
BIRTHDAYS .... ANNIVERSARY ....
ADDRESS ....
....
HOME .... MOBILE ....
EMAIL ....
CHILDREN & BIRTHDAYS ....
....
FAVORITE MEMORY ....
....
....
....
....

NAME ....

BIRTHDAYS .... ANNIVERSARY ....

ADDRESS ....

....

HOME .... MOBILE ....

EMAIL ....

CHILDREN & BIRTHDAYS ....

....

FAVORITE MEMORY ....

....

....

....

....

NAME ....

BIRTHDAYS .... ANNIVERSARY ....

ADDRESS ....

....

HOME .... MOBILE ....

EMAIL ....

CHILDREN & BIRTHDAYS ....

....

FAVORITE MEMORY ....

....

....

....

....

NAME ....
BIRTHDAYS .... ANNIVERSARY ....
ADDRESS ....
....
HOME .... MOBILE ....
EMAIL ....
CHILDREN & BIRTHDAYS ....
....
FAVORITE MEMORY ....
....
....
....
....

NAME ....
BIRTHDAYS .... ANNIVERSARY ....
ADDRESS ....
....
HOME .... MOBILE ....
EMAIL ....
CHILDREN & BIRTHDAYS ....
....
FAVORITE MEMORY ....
....
....
....
....

NAME ....
BIRTHDAYS .... ANNIVERSARY ....
ADDRESS ....
....
HOME .... MOBILE ....
EMAIL ....
CHILDREN & BIRTHDAYS ....
....
FAVORITE MEMORY ....
....
....
....
....

NAME ....
BIRTHDAYS .... ANNIVERSARY ....
ADDRESS ....
....
HOME .... MOBILE ....
EMAIL ....
CHILDREN & BIRTHDAYS ....
....
FAVORITE MEMORY ....
....
....
....
....

NAME ....
BIRTHDAYS .... ANNIVERSARY ....
ADDRESS ....
....
HOME .... MOBILE ....
EMAIL ....
CHILDREN & BIRTHDAYS ....
....
FAVORITE MEMORY ....
....
....
....
....

NAME ....
BIRTHDAYS .... ANNIVERSARY ....
ADDRESS ....
....
HOME .... MOBILE ....
EMAIL ....
CHILDREN & BIRTHDAYS ....
....
FAVORITE MEMORY ....
....
....
....
....

NAME ....

BIRTHDAYS .... ANNIVERSARY ....

ADDRESS ....

....

HOME .... MOBILE ....

EMAIL ....

CHILDREN & BIRTHDAYS ....

....

FAVORITE MEMORY ....

....

....

....

....

NAME ....

BIRTHDAYS .... ANNIVERSARY ....

ADDRESS ....

....

HOME .... MOBILE ....

EMAIL ....

CHILDREN & BIRTHDAYS ....

....

FAVORITE MEMORY ....

....

....

....

....

NAME ....
BIRTHDAYS .... ANNIVERSARY ....
ADDRESS ....
....
HOME .... MOBILE ....
EMAIL ....
CHILDREN & BIRTHDAYS ....
....
FAVORITE MEMORY ....
....
....
....
....

NAME ....
BIRTHDAYS .... ANNIVERSARY ....
ADDRESS ....
....
HOME .... MOBILE ....
EMAIL ....
CHILDREN & BIRTHDAYS ....
....
FAVORITE MEMORY ....
....
....
....
....

NAME ....
BIRTHDAYS .... ANNIVERSARY ....
ADDRESS ....
....

HOME .... MOBILE ....
EMAIL ....
CHILDREN & BIRTHDAYS ....
....
FAVORITE MEMORY ....
....
....
....
....

NAME ....
BIRTHDAYS .... ANNIVERSARY ....
ADDRESS ....
....

HOME .... MOBILE ....
EMAIL ....
CHILDREN & BIRTHDAYS ....
....
FAVORITE MEMORY ....
....
....
....
....

NAME ....

BIRTHDAYS .... ANNIVERSARY ....

ADDRESS ....

....

HOME .... MOBILE ....

EMAIL ....

CHILDREN & BIRTHDAYS ....

....

FAVORITE MEMORY ....

....

....

....

....

NAME ....

BIRTHDAYS .... ANNIVERSARY ....

ADDRESS ....

....

HOME .... MOBILE ....

EMAIL ....

CHILDREN & BIRTHDAYS ....

....

FAVORITE MEMORY ....

....

....

....

....

NAME ....

BIRTHDAYS .... ANNIVERSARY ....

ADDRESS ....

....

HOME .... MOBILE ....

EMAIL ....

CHILDREN & BIRTHDAYS ....

....

FAVORITE MEMORY ....

....

....

....

....

NAME ....

BIRTHDAYS .... ANNIVERSARY ....

ADDRESS ....

....

HOME .... MOBILE ....

EMAIL ....

CHILDREN & BIRTHDAYS ....

....

FAVORITE MEMORY ....

....

....

....

....

NAME ....
BIRTHDAYS .... ANNIVERSARY ....
ADDRESS ....
....
HOME .... MOBILE ....
EMAIL ....
CHILDREN & BIRTHDAYS ....
....
FAVORITE MEMORY ....
....
....
....
....

NAME ....
BIRTHDAYS .... ANNIVERSARY ....
ADDRESS ....
....
HOME .... MOBILE ....
EMAIL ....
CHILDREN & BIRTHDAYS ....
....
FAVORITE MEMORY ....
....
....
....
....

NAME ....
BIRTHDAYS .... ANNIVERSARY ....
ADDRESS ....
....
HOME .... MOBILE ....
EMAIL ....
CHILDREN & BIRTHDAYS ....
....
FAVORITE MEMORY ....
....
....
....
....

NAME ....
BIRTHDAYS .... ANNIVERSARY ....
ADDRESS ....
....
HOME .... MOBILE ....
EMAIL ....
CHILDREN & BIRTHDAYS ....
....
FAVORITE MEMORY ....
....
....
....
....

NAME ....
BIRTHDAYS .... ANNIVERSARY ....
ADDRESS ....
....
HOME .... MOBILE ....
EMAIL ....
CHILDREN & BIRTHDAYS ....
....
FAVORITE MEMORY ....
....
....
....
....

NAME ....
BIRTHDAYS .... ANNIVERSARY ....
ADDRESS ....
....
HOME .... MOBILE ....
EMAIL ....
CHILDREN & BIRTHDAYS ....
....
FAVORITE MEMORY ....
....
....
....
....

NAME ....
BIRTHDAYS .... ANNIVERSARY ....
ADDRESS ....
....
HOME .... MOBILE ....
EMAIL ....
CHILDREN & BIRTHDAYS ....
....
FAVORITE MEMORY ....
....
....
....
....

NAME ....
BIRTHDAYS .... ANNIVERSARY ....
ADDRESS ....
....
HOME .... MOBILE ....
EMAIL ....
CHILDREN & BIRTHDAYS ....
....
FAVORITE MEMORY ....
....
....
....
....

NAME ....
BIRTHDAYS .... ANNIVERSARY ....
ADDRESS ....
....
HOME .... MOBILE ....
EMAIL ....
CHILDREN & BIRTHDAYS ....
....
FAVORITE MEMORY ....
....
....
....
....

NAME ....
BIRTHDAYS .... ANNIVERSARY ....
ADDRESS ....
....
HOME .... MOBILE ....
EMAIL ....
CHILDREN & BIRTHDAYS ....
....
FAVORITE MEMORY ....
....
....
....
....

NAME ....
BIRTHDAYS .... ANNIVERSARY ....
ADDRESS ....
....
HOME .... MOBILE ....
EMAIL ....
CHILDREN & BIRTHDAYS ....
....
FAVORITE MEMORY ....
....
....
....
....

NAME ....
BIRTHDAYS .... ANNIVERSARY ....
ADDRESS ....
....
HOME .... MOBILE ....
EMAIL ....
CHILDREN & BIRTHDAYS ....
....
FAVORITE MEMORY ....
....
....
....
....

NAME ....
BIRTHDAYS .... ANNIVERSARY ....
ADDRESS ....
....
HOME .... MOBILE ....
EMAIL ....
CHILDREN & BIRTHDAYS ....
....
FAVORITE MEMORY ....
....
....
....
....

NAME ....
BIRTHDAYS .... ANNIVERSARY ....
ADDRESS ....
....
HOME .... MOBILE ....
EMAIL ....
CHILDREN & BIRTHDAYS ....
....
FAVORITE MEMORY ....
....
....
....
....

NAME ....

BIRTHDAYS .... ANNIVERSARY ....

ADDRESS ....

....

HOME .... MOBILE ....

EMAIL ....

CHILDREN & BIRTHDAYS ....

....

FAVORITE MEMORY ....

....

....

....

....

NAME ....

BIRTHDAYS .... ANNIVERSARY ....

ADDRESS ....

....

HOME .... MOBILE ....

EMAIL ....

CHILDREN & BIRTHDAYS ....

....

FAVORITE MEMORY ....

....

....

....

....

NAME ....
BIRTHDAYS .... ANNIVERSARY ....
ADDRESS ....
....
HOME .... MOBILE ....
EMAIL ....
CHILDREN & BIRTHDAYS ....
....
FAVORITE MEMORY ....
....
....
....
....

NAME ....
BIRTHDAYS .... ANNIVERSARY ....
ADDRESS ....
....
HOME .... MOBILE ....
EMAIL ....
CHILDREN & BIRTHDAYS ....
....
FAVORITE MEMORY ....
....
....
....
....

NAME ....

BIRTHDAYS .... ANNIVERSARY ....

ADDRESS ....

....

HOME .... MOBILE ....

EMAIL ....

CHILDREN & BIRTHDAYS ....

....

FAVORITE MEMORY ....

....

....

....

....

NAME ....

BIRTHDAYS .... ANNIVERSARY ....

ADDRESS ....

....

HOME .... MOBILE ....

EMAIL ....

CHILDREN & BIRTHDAYS ....

....

FAVORITE MEMORY ....

....

....

....

....

NAME ....

BIRTHDAYS .... ANNIVERSARY ....

ADDRESS ....

....

HOME .... MOBILE ....

EMAIL ....

CHILDREN & BIRTHDAYS ....

....

FAVORITE MEMORY ....

....

....

....

....

NAME ....

BIRTHDAYS .... ANNIVERSARY ....

ADDRESS ....

....

HOME .... MOBILE ....

EMAIL ....

CHILDREN & BIRTHDAYS ....

....

FAVORITE MEMORY ....

....

....

....

....

NAME ....

BIRTHDAYS .... ANNIVERSARY ....

ADDRESS ....

....

HOME .... MOBILE ....

EMAIL ....

CHILDREN & BIRTHDAYS ....

....

FAVORITE MEMORY ....

....

....

....

....

NAME ....

BIRTHDAYS .... ANNIVERSARY ....

ADDRESS ....

....

HOME .... MOBILE ....

EMAIL ....

CHILDREN & BIRTHDAYS ....

....

FAVORITE MEMORY ....

....

....

....

....

NAME ....

BIRTHDAYS .... ANNIVERSARY ....

ADDRESS ....

....

HOME .... MOBILE ....

EMAIL ....

CHILDREN & BIRTHDAYS ....

....

FAVORITE MEMORY ....

....

....

....

....

NAME ....

BIRTHDAYS .... ANNIVERSARY ....

ADDRESS ....

....

HOME .... MOBILE ....

EMAIL ....

CHILDREN & BIRTHDAYS ....

....

FAVORITE MEMORY ....

....

....

....

....

NAME ....
BIRTHDAYS .... ANNIVERSARY ....
ADDRESS ....
....
HOME .... MOBILE ....
EMAIL ....
CHILDREN & BIRTHDAYS ....
....
FAVORITE MEMORY ....
....
....
....
....

NAME ....
BIRTHDAYS .... ANNIVERSARY ....
ADDRESS ....
....
HOME .... MOBILE ....
EMAIL ....
CHILDREN & BIRTHDAYS ....
....
FAVORITE MEMORY ....
....
....
....
....

NAME ....
BIRTHDAYS .... ANNIVERSARY ....
ADDRESS ....
....
HOME .... MOBILE ....
EMAIL ....
CHILDREN & BIRTHDAYS ....
....
FAVORITE MEMORY ....
....
....
....
....

NAME ....
BIRTHDAYS .... ANNIVERSARY ....
ADDRESS ....
....
HOME .... MOBILE ....
EMAIL ....
CHILDREN & BIRTHDAYS ....
....
FAVORITE MEMORY ....
....
....
....
....

NAME . . . .
BIRTHDAYS . . . . ANNIVERSARY . . . .
ADDRESS . . . .

. . . .

HOME . . . . MOBILE . . . .
EMAIL . . . .
CHILDREN & BIRTHDAYS . . . .

. . . .

FAVORITE MEMORY . . . .

. . . .

. . . .

. . . .

. . . .

NAME . . . .
BIRTHDAYS . . . . ANNIVERSARY . . . .
ADDRESS . . . .

. . . .

HOME . . . . MOBILE . . . .
EMAIL . . . .
CHILDREN & BIRTHDAYS . . . .

. . . .

FAVORITE MEMORY . . . .

. . . .

. . . .

. . . .

. . . .

NAME ....

BIRTHDAYS .... ANNIVERSARY ....

ADDRESS ....

....

HOME .... MOBILE ....

EMAIL ....

CHILDREN & BIRTHDAYS ....

....

FAVORITE MEMORY ....

....

....

....

....

NAME ....

BIRTHDAYS .... ANNIVERSARY ....

ADDRESS ....

....

HOME .... MOBILE ....

EMAIL ....

CHILDREN & BIRTHDAYS ....

....

FAVORITE MEMORY ....

....

....

....

NAME ....

BIRTHDAYS .... ANNIVERSARY ....

ADDRESS ....

....

HOME .... MOBILE ....

EMAIL ....

CHILDREN & BIRTHDAYS ....

....

FAVORITE MEMORY ....

....

....

....

....

NAME ....

BIRTHDAYS .... ANNIVERSARY ....

ADDRESS ....

....

HOME .... MOBILE ....

EMAIL ....

CHILDREN & BIRTHDAYS ....

....

FAVORITE MEMORY ....

....

....

....

....

NAME ....
BIRTHDAYS .... ANNIVERSARY ....
ADDRESS ....
....
HOME .... MOBILE ....
EMAIL ....
CHILDREN & BIRTHDAYS ....
....
FAVORITE MEMORY ....
....
....
....
....

NAME ....
BIRTHDAYS .... ANNIVERSARY ....
ADDRESS ....
....
HOME .... MOBILE ....
EMAIL ....
CHILDREN & BIRTHDAYS ....
....
FAVORITE MEMORY ....
....
....
....
....

NAME ....
BIRTHDAYS .... ANNIVERSARY ....
ADDRESS ....
....
HOME .... MOBILE ....
EMAIL ....
CHILDREN & BIRTHDAYS ....
....
FAVORITE MEMORY ....
....
....
....
....
....

NAME ....
BIRTHDAYS .... ANNIVERSARY ....
ADDRESS ....
....
HOME .... MOBILE ....
EMAIL ....
CHILDREN & BIRTHDAYS ....
....
FAVORITE MEMORY ....
....
....
....
....
....

NAME ....
BIRTHDAYS .... ANNIVERSARY ....
ADDRESS ....
....
HOME .... MOBILE ....
EMAIL ....
CHILDREN & BIRTHDAYS ....
....
FAVORITE MEMORY ....
....
....
....
....

NAME ....
BIRTHDAYS .... ANNIVERSARY ....
ADDRESS ....
....
HOME .... MOBILE ....
EMAIL ....
CHILDREN & BIRTHDAYS ....
....
FAVORITE MEMORY ....
....
....
....
....

NAME . . . .
BIRTHDAYS . . . . ANNIVERSARY . . . .
ADDRESS . . . .
. . . .
HOME . . . . MOBILE . . . .
EMAIL . . . .
CHILDREN & BIRTHDAYS . . . .
. . . .
FAVORITE MEMORY . . . .
. . . .
. . . .
. . . .
. . . .

NAME . . . .
BIRTHDAYS . . . . ANNIVERSARY . . . .
ADDRESS . . . .
. . . .
HOME . . . . MOBILE . . . .
EMAIL . . . .
CHILDREN & BIRTHDAYS . . . .
. . . .
FAVORITE MEMORY . . . .
. . . .
. . . .
. . . .
. . . .

NAME ....

BIRTHDAYS .... ANNIVERSARY ....

ADDRESS ....

....

HOME .... MOBILE ....

EMAIL ....

CHILDREN & BIRTHDAYS ....

....

FAVORITE MEMORY ....

....

....

....

....

NAME ....

BIRTHDAYS .... ANNIVERSARY ....

ADDRESS ....

....

HOME .... MOBILE ....

EMAIL ....

CHILDREN & BIRTHDAYS ....

....

FAVORITE MEMORY ....

....

....

....

....

NAME ....

BIRTHDAYS .... ANNIVERSARY ....

ADDRESS ....

....

HOME .... MOBILE ....

EMAIL ....

CHILDREN & BIRTHDAYS ....

....

FAVORITE MEMORY ....

....

....

....

....

NAME ....

BIRTHDAYS .... ANNIVERSARY ....

ADDRESS ....

....

HOME .... MOBILE ....

EMAIL ....

CHILDREN & BIRTHDAYS ....

....

FAVORITE MEMORY ....

....

....

....

....

NAME ....
BIRTHDAYS .... ANNIVERSARY ....
ADDRESS ....
....
HOME .... MOBILE ....
EMAIL ....
CHILDREN & BIRTHDAYS ....
....
FAVORITE MEMORY ....
....
....
....
....

NAME ....
BIRTHDAYS .... ANNIVERSARY ....
ADDRESS ....
....
HOME .... MOBILE ....
EMAIL ....
CHILDREN & BIRTHDAYS ....
....
FAVORITE MEMORY ....
....
....
....
....

NAME ....
BIRTHDAYS .... ANNIVERSARY ....
ADDRESS ....
....

HOME .... MOBILE ....
EMAIL ....
CHILDREN & BIRTHDAYS ....
....
FAVORITE MEMORY ....
....
....
....
....

NAME ....
BIRTHDAYS .... ANNIVERSARY ....
ADDRESS ....
....

HOME .... MOBILE ....
EMAIL ....
CHILDREN & BIRTHDAYS ....
....
FAVORITE MEMORY ....
....
....
....
....

NAME ....
BIRTHDAYS .... ANNIVERSARY ....
ADDRESS ....
....
HOME .... MOBILE ....
EMAIL ....
CHILDREN & BIRTHDAYS ....
....
FAVORITE MEMORY ....
....
....
....
....

NAME ....
BIRTHDAYS .... ANNIVERSARY ....
ADDRESS ....
....
HOME .... MOBILE ....
EMAIL ....
CHILDREN & BIRTHDAYS ....
....
FAVORITE MEMORY ....
....
....
....
....

NAME . . . .
BIRTHDAYS . . . . ANNIVERSARY . . . .
ADDRESS . . . .
. . . .
HOME . . . . MOBILE . . . .
EMAIL . . . .
CHILDREN & BIRTHDAYS . . . .
. . . .
FAVORITE MEMORY . . . .
. . . .
. . . .
. . . .
. . . .

NAME . . . .
BIRTHDAYS . . . . ANNIVERSARY . . . .
ADDRESS . . . .
. . . .
HOME . . . . MOBILE . . . .
EMAIL . . . .
CHILDREN & BIRTHDAYS . . . .
. . . .
FAVORITE MEMORY . . . .
. . . .
. . . .
. . . .
. . . .

NAME ....
BIRTHDAYS .... ANNIVERSARY ....
ADDRESS ....
....
HOME .... MOBILE ....
EMAIL ....
CHILDREN & BIRTHDAYS ....
....
FAVORITE MEMORY ....
....
....
....

NAME ....
BIRTHDAYS .... ANNIVERSARY ....
ADDRESS ....
....
HOME .... MOBILE ....
EMAIL ....
CHILDREN & BIRTHDAYS ....
....
FAVORITE MEMORY ....
....
....
....

NAME ....
BIRTHDAYS .... ANNIVERSARY ....
ADDRESS ....
....
HOME .... MOBILE ....
EMAIL ....
CHILDREN & BIRTHDAYS ....
....
FAVORITE MEMORY ....
....
....
....
....

NAME ....
BIRTHDAYS .... ANNIVERSARY ....
ADDRESS ....
....
HOME .... MOBILE ....
EMAIL ....
CHILDREN & BIRTHDAYS ....
....
FAVORITE MEMORY ....
....
....
....
....

NAME ....
BIRTHDAYS .... ANNIVERSARY ....
ADDRESS ....
....
HOME .... MOBILE ....
EMAIL ....
CHILDREN & BIRTHDAYS ....
....
FAVORITE MEMORY ....
....
....
....
....

NAME ....
BIRTHDAYS .... ANNIVERSARY ....
ADDRESS ....
....
HOME .... MOBILE ....
EMAIL ....
CHILDREN & BIRTHDAYS ....
....
FAVORITE MEMORY ....
....
....
....
....

NAME ....
BIRTHDAYS .... ANNIVERSARY ....
ADDRESS ....
....

HOME .... MOBILE ....
EMAIL ....
CHILDREN & BIRTHDAYS ....
....
FAVORITE MEMORY ....
....
....
....
....

NAME ....
BIRTHDAYS .... ANNIVERSARY ....
ADDRESS ....
....

HOME .... MOBILE ....
EMAIL ....
CHILDREN & BIRTHDAYS ....
....
FAVORITE MEMORY ....
....
....
....
....

NAME ....
BIRTHDAYS .... ANNIVERSARY ....
ADDRESS ....
....
HOME .... MOBILE ....
EMAIL ....
CHILDREN & BIRTHDAYS ....
....
FAVORITE MEMORY ....
....
....
....
....

NAME ....
BIRTHDAYS .... ANNIVERSARY ....
ADDRESS ....
....
HOME .... MOBILE ....
EMAIL ....
CHILDREN & BIRTHDAYS ....
....
FAVORITE MEMORY ....
....
....
....

NAME ....

BIRTHDAYS .... ANNIVERSARY ....

ADDRESS ....

....

HOME .... MOBILE ....

EMAIL ....

CHILDREN & BIRTHDAYS ....

....

FAVORITE MEMORY ....

....

....

....

....

NAME ....

BIRTHDAYS .... ANNIVERSARY ....

ADDRESS ....

....

HOME .... MOBILE ....

EMAIL ....

CHILDREN & BIRTHDAYS ....

....

FAVORITE MEMORY ....

....

....

....

....

NAME ....
BIRTHDAYS .... ANNIVERSARY ....
ADDRESS ....
....
HOME .... MOBILE ....
EMAIL ....
CHILDREN & BIRTHDAYS ....
....
FAVORITE MEMORY ....
....
....
....
....

NAME ....
BIRTHDAYS .... ANNIVERSARY ....
ADDRESS ....
....
HOME .... MOBILE ....
EMAIL ....
CHILDREN & BIRTHDAYS ....
....
FAVORITE MEMORY ....
....
....
....
....

NAME ....

BIRTHDAYS .... ANNIVERSARY ....

ADDRESS ....

....

HOME .... MOBILE ....

EMAIL ....

CHILDREN & BIRTHDAYS ....

....

FAVORITE MEMORY ....

....

....

....

....

NAME ....

BIRTHDAYS .... ANNIVERSARY ....

ADDRESS ....

....

HOME .... MOBILE ....

EMAIL ....

CHILDREN & BIRTHDAYS ....

....

FAVORITE MEMORY ....

....

....

....

....

NAME . . . .
BIRTHDAYS . . . . ANNIVERSARY . . . .
ADDRESS . . . .
. . . .
HOME . . . . MOBILE . . . .
EMAIL . . . .
CHILDREN & BIRTHDAYS . . . .
. . . .
FAVORITE MEMORY . . . .
. . . .
. . . .
. . . .
. . . .

NAME . . . .
BIRTHDAYS . . . . ANNIVERSARY . . . .
ADDRESS . . . .
. . . .
HOME . . . . MOBILE . . . .
EMAIL . . . .
CHILDREN & BIRTHDAYS . . . .
. . . .
FAVORITE MEMORY . . . .
. . . .
. . . .
. . . .
. . . .

NAME ....
BIRTHDAYS .... ANNIVERSARY ....
ADDRESS ....
....
HOME .... MOBILE ....
EMAIL ....
CHILDREN & BIRTHDAYS ....
....
FAVORITE MEMORY ....
....
....
....
....

NAME ....
BIRTHDAYS .... ANNIVERSARY ....
ADDRESS ....
....
HOME .... MOBILE ....
EMAIL ....
CHILDREN & BIRTHDAYS ....
....
FAVORITE MEMORY ....
....
....
....
....

NAME ....
BIRTHDAYS .... ANNIVERSARY ....
ADDRESS ....
....
HOME .... MOBILE ....
EMAIL ....
CHILDREN & BIRTHDAYS ....
....
FAVORITE MEMORY ....
....
....
....
....

NAME ....
BIRTHDAYS .... ANNIVERSARY ....
ADDRESS ....
....
HOME .... MOBILE ....
EMAIL ....
CHILDREN & BIRTHDAYS ....
....
FAVORITE MEMORY ....
....
....
....

NAME ....
BIRTHDAYS .... ANNIVERSARY ....
ADDRESS ....
....
HOME .... MOBILE ....
EMAIL ....
CHILDREN & BIRTHDAYS ....
....
FAVORITE MEMORY ....
....
....
....
....

NAME ....
BIRTHDAYS .... ANNIVERSARY ....
ADDRESS ....
....
HOME .... MOBILE ....
EMAIL ....
CHILDREN & BIRTHDAYS ....
....
FAVORITE MEMORY ....
....
....
....
....

NAME ....
BIRTHDAYS .... ANNIVERSARY ....
ADDRESS ....
....
HOME .... MOBILE ....
EMAIL ....
CHILDREN & BIRTHDAYS ....
....
FAVORITE MEMORY ....
....
....
....
....

NAME ....
BIRTHDAYS .... ANNIVERSARY ....
ADDRESS ....
....
HOME .... MOBILE ....
EMAIL ....
CHILDREN & BIRTHDAYS ....
....
FAVORITE MEMORY ....
....
....
....

NAME ....
BIRTHDAYS .... ANNIVERSARY ....
ADDRESS ....
....
HOME .... MOBILE ....
EMAIL ....
CHILDREN & BIRTHDAYS ....
....
FAVORITE MEMORY ....
....
....
....
....

NAME ....
BIRTHDAYS .... ANNIVERSARY ....
ADDRESS ....
....
HOME .... MOBILE ....
EMAIL ....
CHILDREN & BIRTHDAYS ....
....
FAVORITE MEMORY ....
....
....
....
....

NAME ....
BIRTHDAYS .... ANNIVERSARY ....
ADDRESS ....
....
HOME .... MOBILE ....
EMAIL ....
CHILDREN & BIRTHDAYS ....
....
FAVORITE MEMORY ....
....
....
....
....

NAME ....
BIRTHDAYS .... ANNIVERSARY ....
ADDRESS ....
....
HOME .... MOBILE ....
EMAIL ....
CHILDREN & BIRTHDAYS ....
....
FAVORITE MEMORY ....
....
....
....

NAME ....

BIRTHDAYS .... ANNIVERSARY ....

ADDRESS ....

....

HOME .... MOBILE ....

EMAIL ....

CHILDREN & BIRTHDAYS ....

....

FAVORITE MEMORY ....

....

....

....

....

NAME ....

BIRTHDAYS .... ANNIVERSARY ....

ADDRESS ....

....

HOME .... MOBILE ....

EMAIL ....

CHILDREN & BIRTHDAYS ....

....

FAVORITE MEMORY ....

....

....

....

NAME ....
BIRTHDAYS .... ANNIVERSARY ....
ADDRESS ....
....
HOME .... MOBILE ....
EMAIL ....
CHILDREN & BIRTHDAYS ....
....
FAVORITE MEMORY ....
....
....
....
....

NAME ....
BIRTHDAYS .... ANNIVERSARY ....
ADDRESS ....
....
HOME .... MOBILE ....
EMAIL ....
CHILDREN & BIRTHDAYS ....
....
FAVORITE MEMORY ....
....
....
....

NAME ....
BIRTHDAYS .... ANNIVERSARY ....
ADDRESS ....
....

HOME .... MOBILE ....
EMAIL ....
CHILDREN & BIRTHDAYS ....
....
FAVORITE MEMORY ....
....
....
....
....

NAME ....
BIRTHDAYS .... ANNIVERSARY ....
ADDRESS ....
....

HOME .... MOBILE ....
EMAIL ....
CHILDREN & BIRTHDAYS ....
....
FAVORITE MEMORY ....
....
....
....
....

NAME ....
BIRTHDAYS .... ANNIVERSARY ....
ADDRESS ....
....
HOME .... MOBILE ....
EMAIL ....
CHILDREN & BIRTHDAYS ....
....
FAVORITE MEMORY ....
....
....
....
....

NAME ....
BIRTHDAYS .... ANNIVERSARY ....
ADDRESS ....
....
HOME .... MOBILE ....
EMAIL ....
CHILDREN & BIRTHDAYS ....
....
FAVORITE MEMORY ....
....
....
....
....

NAME ....
BIRTHDAYS .... ANNIVERSARY ....
ADDRESS ....
....
HOME .... MOBILE ....
EMAIL ....
CHILDREN & BIRTHDAYS ....
....
FAVORITE MEMORY ....
....
....
....
....

NAME ....
BIRTHDAYS .... ANNIVERSARY ....
ADDRESS ....
....
HOME .... MOBILE ....
EMAIL ....
CHILDREN & BIRTHDAYS ....
....
FAVORITE MEMORY ....
....
....
....
....

NAME ....
BIRTHDAYS .... ANNIVERSARY ....
ADDRESS ....
....
HOME .... MOBILE ....
EMAIL ....
CHILDREN & BIRTHDAYS ....
....
FAVORITE MEMORY ....
....
....
....
....

NAME ....
BIRTHDAYS .... ANNIVERSARY ....
ADDRESS ....
....
HOME .... MOBILE ....
EMAIL ....
CHILDREN & BIRTHDAYS ....
....
FAVORITE MEMORY ....
....
....
....
....

NAME ....

BIRTHDAYS .... ANNIVERSARY ....

ADDRESS ....

....

HOME .... MOBILE ....

EMAIL ....

CHILDREN & BIRTHDAYS ....

....

FAVORITE MEMORY ....

....

....

....

....

NAME ....

BIRTHDAYS .... ANNIVERSARY ....

ADDRESS ....

....

HOME .... MOBILE ....

EMAIL ....

CHILDREN & BIRTHDAYS ....

....

FAVORITE MEMORY ....

....

....

....

....

NAME ....
BIRTHDAYS .... ANNIVERSARY ....
ADDRESS ....
....
HOME .... MOBILE ....
EMAIL ....
CHILDREN & BIRTHDAYS ....
....
FAVORITE MEMORY ....
....
....
....
....

NAME ....
BIRTHDAYS .... ANNIVERSARY ....
ADDRESS ....
....
HOME .... MOBILE ....
EMAIL ....
CHILDREN & BIRTHDAYS ....
....
FAVORITE MEMORY ....
....
....
....

NAME ....

BIRTHDAYS .... ANNIVERSARY ....

ADDRESS ....

....

HOME .... MOBILE ....

EMAIL ....

CHILDREN & BIRTHDAYS ....

....

FAVORITE MEMORY ....

....

....

....

....

NAME ....

BIRTHDAYS .... ANNIVERSARY ....

ADDRESS ....

....

HOME .... MOBILE ....

EMAIL ....

CHILDREN & BIRTHDAYS ....

....

FAVORITE MEMORY ....

....

....

....

....

NAME ....
BIRTHDAYS .... ANNIVERSARY ....
ADDRESS ....
....
HOME .... MOBILE ....
EMAIL ....
CHILDREN & BIRTHDAYS ....
....
FAVORITE MEMORY ....
....
....
....
....

NAME ....
BIRTHDAYS .... ANNIVERSARY ....
ADDRESS ....
....
HOME .... MOBILE ....
EMAIL ....
CHILDREN & BIRTHDAYS ....
....
FAVORITE MEMORY ....
....
....
....
....

Celebrating Families

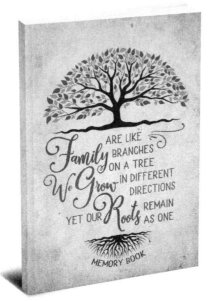

You might also like the matching 6" x 9" Memory Book

We hope you enjoyed using this book.
It would really help us a lot if you would
take a moment to leave a review.
Thanks!

. . . .

Guestbooks For Every Occasion
Check out all of our guestbooks at:
amazon.com/author/guestbooksforeveryoccasion

Made in the USA
Monee, IL
15 May 2021